GREAT AMERICAN
SMOOTHIES

GREAT AMERICAN
SMOOTHIES

GABRIEL CONSTANS

Avery Publishing Group
Garden City Park, New York

Cover Design: William Gonzalez and Rudy Shur
Cover Photo: Envision, New York, NY
Text Illustrator: John Wincek
In-House Editor: Jennifer L. Santo
Typesetter: Elaine V. McCaw
Printer: Paragon Press, Honesdale, PA

Avery Publishing Group
120 Old Broadway
Garden City Park, NY 11040
1-800-548-5757

Library of Congress Cataloging-in-Publication Data

Constans, Gabriel.
    Great American smoothies : the ultimate blending guide for shakes,
slushes, desserts & thirst quenchers / Gabriel Constans.
           p.   cm.
      Includes index.
      ISBN 0-89529-784-1
      1. Blenders (Cookery) I.Title.
TX840.B5c67 1997   97-7712
641.5'89—dc21   CIP

Printed in the United States of America

10   9   8   7   6

Contents

This book is dedicated to my partner, Audrey, and my children, Shona, Brendon, Jason, Darci, and Leti, who provided fertile ground and inspiration for my smoothie research and creation.

Preface

In 1980, when my first child was born, I began look-ing for a food or drink that would be both nourishing and tasteful for my daughter. In the process, I discov-ered the smoothie. Since then, many combinations and recipes have been created for our children and friends, young and old alike. Increasing pressure from these legions of friends and family for an in-depth compilation of my smoothie secrets prompted the cre-ation of what you now hold in your excited hands. For months, I surrounded myself with smoothies. I woke, worked, slept, dreamed, and breathed smoothies morning, noon, and night to bring these time- and human-tested marvels into your life.

Smoothies provide a healthy, timely alternative to the "quick-fix," grease- and cholesterol-saturated foods that are so common in the American diet. They can be concocted at any time of the year for you and your fam-ily's enjoyment. They're formulated to pique your interest and not only enhance your health and change your life, but also bring a smile to your face and put a twinkle in your eye. Smoothies put a little spark in your life. If your life is already sparked, they help ignite it! And if your fire's been lit for some time, they keep it burning.

It only takes five to ten minutes to make your favorite drink. A quick smoothie breakfast, lunch, dinner, snack, or dessert can be prepared with little fuss or bother. Smoothies are an excellent supplement to any meal or diet. And if you're really in a rush, you can take them with you.

Smoothies are not only full of life, they also taste fantastic! Babies, toddlers, children, teenagers, and adults find them to be absolutely delicious. Ingredients that many children would shun if they were presented separately are eagerly devoured in smoothie form. Teenagers and adults enjoy the variety of flavors and the potential to create a distinct smoothie to match their style and taste preference.

Smoothies are not just a West Coast fad. They have been around, in one form or another, for many years throughout the world, and are once again beginning to enjoy widespread popularity. Walk through any upscale food court mall and, chances are, you'll find a smoothie shop. These smoothies make great snacks, but make sure the shop doesn't add any thickeners or large amounts of sugar. If you're not sure about this, ask.

Of course, as is the case with most foods, there is no substitute for the fresh, organic, healthy smoothies you make yourself. Here are some recipes to get you started.

Introduction

The Smoothie is Born

Long ago and far away, in the land of hither and yon, there lived a legendary goddess. She wasn't your average, run-of-the-mill goddess; she didn't rule the earth, fire, love, or other elemental realms, but her magic surpassed that of all other gods. She was the keeper of the Original Smoothie Recipe.

Without her intervention, human beings would have remained in darkness. Out of her immense compassion, the greatest potion ever tasted by mortals was revealed. This extraordinary event, which changed drinking history forever, came to pass in the year 1981.

It went something like this. . .

After months of frustration with unwholesome, commercial baby food, a man bade farewell to his family and friends and embarked on a perilous journey. He would travel to the ends of the earth to find a healthy food alternative for his one-and-a-half-year-old daughter, one without sweeteners, chemicals, or food coloring.

He traveled countless miles through the desert, over the mountains, and across the sea, until he finally arrived at a cave in the deepest jungle of Freedonia. It was in the recesses of this dark cave that he began to contemplate his predicament—he was dying of thirst.

He repeated the essential question out loud again and again: "Is there anything to drink around here?"

After three days of thirst his throat was parched, his legs ached, and his mind began to wander. Suddenly, in the soft darkness of the cave, he heard a faint, soothing voice calling softly, "Smoothies . . . Smooooothies . . . Smooooooooooothies."

"Who's there?" asked the enthralled and terrified man.

As he rubbed his eyes, there appeared before him a goddess in the shape of a swirling, ten-foot-tall, ripe banana.

"I am the one and only. I am the great, incredible, spectacular, stupendous, outrageous, long-winded Smoothie Goddess."

"Well, of course you are. Anyone could see that," he replied. And then he asked the earthshaking question, "What in heaven's name is a smoothie?"

She glared at him as only a Smoothie Goddess can and said, "You mean you don't know?" Then she remembered that she had been playing solitaire for eons and hadn't told anyone her secrets. After so many years alone in a cave, you start to forget things.

"I'm sorry," she said. "Of course you don't know. How could you?"

Without further hesitation, she revealed to him the secret potion of the gods—the smoothie. She instructed him in all facets of the art of preparing smoothies. (A blender, refrigerator, and electrical socket were conveniently located in the back of the cave, and powered by a solar panel outside.) She made him solemnly promise to reveal her smoothie secrets to all the people of the earth, and no one else.

After a week of intense instruction, the man returned to his home. From that moment on, everyone who met him could feel the presence of the goddess within him. Day after day, he blended his secret concoctions for babies, children, young adults, and grown-ups. His life was filled with peace and happiness as his recipes spread throughout the world's kitchens.

He continues to share the secrets entrusted to him by the great Smoothie Goddess with all who seek the essence of cool refreshment. The legend of this historical event continues. Disciples of the Smoothie Goddess are being initiated on a daily basis. The man's vision of the goddess in a cave, far from home, was the beginning of a never-ending story.

Proper Smoothie Etiquette

(Or, Everything You Wanted to Know About Smoothies, But Were Afraid to Ask)

The following information is indispensible for virgin smoothie drinkers, and should answer any embarrassing questions you may have about this refreshing treat.

What is the Best Position in Which to Drink a Smoothie?

Sitting, standing, kneeling, crawling, reclining, stretching, and leaning against a wall are the most common positions in which to drink your favorite smoothie. Lying on your back, sleeping, singing, or running while drinking a smoothie are advanced techniques that should not be attempted without the help of a professional.

Where and When Can I Drink My Smoothie?

Anywhere and at any time. The most common locations are in the house, on the porch, or in a restaurant. People have also been observed knocking back smoothies at the beach; in planes, cars, tunnels, and skyscrapers; on boats, trains, bikes, and skateboards; while surfing; on mountaintops and rivers; in deserts and valleys; while hiking, skiing, working, and swimming; in bathrooms, showers, movie theaters, trees, and closets; over and under beds; as part of lovemaking; and at the White House, the Pentagon, the Olympics, and the United Nations Security Council.

What Should I Wear?

Before drinking a smoothie, special care should be given to your wardrobe. The most widely-used dress consists of shorts, a short-sleeved shirt, and sandals. Bare feet and no shirt are also common. Other acceptable attire includes bathing suits, casual dress, formal wear, or the smoothie lover's favorite, nothing at all!

Various hats can add a special flair to your smoothie-drinking attire. A bowler gives you that distinguished English look, while a baseball hat or football helmet lets everyone know you're a macho, jock kind of smoothier. One of my favorites is the Dick Tracy or Humphrey Bogart detective fedora. And of course, there are always those smoothie drinkers who go for that uniform appearance, with police officers', nurses', and firefighters' caps.

Are Smoothies Healthy, As Well As Tasty and Fun?

Absolutely! When made with the right blend of ingredients—such as fresh fruits or vegetables—smoothies can be a great source of vitamins, minerals, enzymes, and other nutrients. (Of course, you don't have to tell your kids this!) Examples of healthy-but-tasty smoothies include the Morning Lift-Off on page 23, the Bird of Paradise on page 56, or any of the smoothies in Chapter 5. Just remember to use organically grown fruits and vegetables wherever possible. If these are not readily available, make sure you clean your produce thoroughly to wash off any residual dirt or pesticides.

How Do You Taste a Smoothie?
How Can you Judge Its Age, Contents, or Flavor?

Smoothie-tasting is an acquired art that takes skill, patience, and ESP (Elementary Spiritual Powers). You must be highly motivated to learn these techniques—or have nothing better to do. There are no right answers, of course. This is not a test, but an exercise for the true smoothie enthusiast.

Texture. After pouring your smoothie into a tall, clear, clean glass, you must first observe its texture. Is it thick or thin? Does it pour slowly, or is it runny? Will it hold up under pressure, or melt like ice?

Color. Next is the color. Is your smoothie red, orange, green, black, pink, or a rainbow of colors? Does the color change with time? Is the top of the drink a different color than the bottom?

Sound. Once you've ascertained its texture and color, you should then begin to listen to your smoothie. Yes, listen!

Hold the glass up to your ear—either one—and swirl it around. Do you hear anything? If not, you may be hard of hearing. Check the other ear, or have someone else listen.

You must listen for an entire thirty seconds to get the full effect; any longer and your arm gets tired swirling the glass around. After half a minute you will begin to hear the essence of the smoothie. Some people have heard angels, some a babbling brook, and still others an erupting volcano! If you hear voices, see a psychiatrist or guru immediately.

A new recording of natural environmental sounds will soon be released which includes a smoothie track for relaxation and stress reduction.

Smell. Now you have come to a critical phase of smoothie-tasting. Once you've observed the texture, color, and sound of your smoothie, you must smell it!

Hold the glass under your nose. Put the middle finger of your right hand (or left hand, for lefties) in the middle of your forehead. Press the thumb of the same hand in on your right nostril, closing off that nasal passage. Breathe slowly through your left nostril with four slow, deep breaths. Repeat with your opposite hand, closing your left nostril and breathing through your right with four slow, deep breaths. Remove your fingers from both nostrils and forehead and take one very long, deep, full breath with your nose directly over the glass. Hold that breath as long as possible, then slowly exhale.

If you pass out, make sure to place your smoothie on a stable surface before falling. Also, beware of others stealing your smoothie when you're unconscious.

Tasting. Last, but not least, you have arrived at the climactic conclusion of your smoothie-drinking preliminaries.

Take one finger (any one will do). Make sure it is clean (unless you prefer some organic or chemical matter blended in), and place it directly and slowly into the middle of your drink. Do not touch the side of the glass.

Remove your finger carefully and place it immediately on your tongue or that of a loved one. Suck the smoothie off your finger with eyes closed; let the taste linger.

Wah La! (or, as the French say, "Voilà!") You are now ready to indulge in your new favorite pastime and future addiction. Commence draining the remainder of your succulent liquid with unbearable joy and ecstasy!

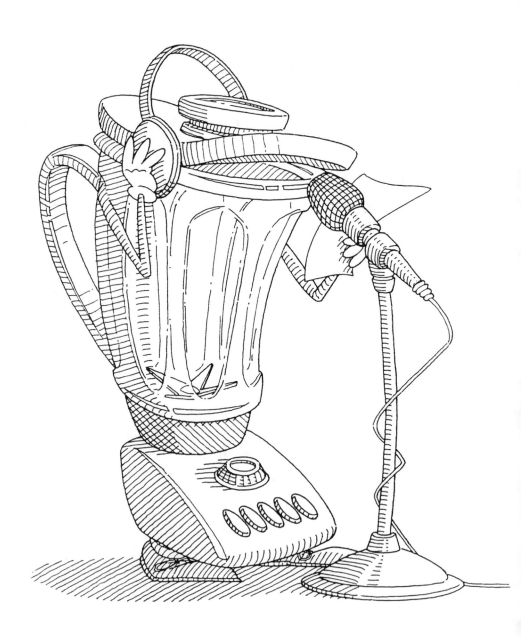

A Word About Blenders

Blenders have been around since the 1930s, when Stephen J. Poplawski designed a contraption to stir a malted milk shake. Since that time, designs have come and gone, but the fundamentals remain.

Blenders have a variety of speeds, controls, and features. The most important aspects, however, are a good motor, a stainless steel blade, and a wide range of speed.

Plastic pitchers are lighter and easier to handle than glass, although some feel that glass holds up better in washing and provides less opportunity for contamination from the plastic. Wide-mouth containers are easiest to clean, and markings on all containers are a must to help in measuring.

Prices for a standard blender run between $20 and $70. You can usually find a medium-priced model with a strong motor for around $35 to $45. The cheaper models with weaker motors tend to burn out quickly.

Remember, for smoothies you need only a standard blender, not a juicer or food processor. If you don't want to spend the money for a standard blender, a hand blender will work just as well, and costs about $20.

You can, of course, opt for the do-it-yourself manual mixer. This works by placing the ingredients into a large glass with a tight-fitting lid, and rolling, shaking, and jumping up and down for days. The side effects are somewhat daunting, however, and most people end up forking out a few bucks for an electric blender.

Ingredients

Most of the ingredients used in the smoothie recipes in this book should already be in your kitchen cabinet, or available at your local grocery store. However, there may be some which are unfamiliar to you. Here are some explanations of these ingredients, and hints on where they can be obtained.

Almond butter. Similar to peanut butter, but made from almonds. Almonds are a good source of B complex vitamins, calcium, phosphorus, iron, potassium, and protein. Almond butter is available in natural food stores and some major supermarkets.

Brewer's yeast. Contains zinc, iron, and B complex vitamins.

Brown rice syrup. A sweetener made from rice, which retains some of the nutrients of the rice. It is mildly sweet, with a light malt flavor, and can be used in place of honey. It is obtainable in most natural food stores.

Carob powder. This is an alternative to milk chocolate that is made from the pods of an evergreen tree. Carob is high in minerals, but low in fat, and contains no caffeine. It tastes similar to chocolate, but it is naturally sweet, so less sweetener is needed in recipes which contain carob. It can be bought in bulk at natural food stores.

Chai. Traditional Indian spiced tea. It can be bought prepackaged at natural food stores or made at home by combining equal amounts of cinnamon, nutmeg, ginger, cloves, dates, and cardamom. Add 8 cups water, bring the mixture to a boil, and simmer for 20 minutes.

Coconut milk. Liquid from the center of the coconut, available canned at most markets. You could use fresh coconut, but you would need at least four to obtain the desired quantity, and they are difficult to crack.

Egg substitute. Egg substitute is a blend of stabilizers and raising ingredients in a gluten-free base, and should contain no egg or animal protein. It is useful for people who are trying to limit their cholesterol intake. 1 1/2 teaspoons of egg substitute mixed with 2 tablespoons of water equals 1 egg. Egg substitute is available in most supermarkets.

Filtered water. Tap water often contains harmful chemicals, parasites, and lead, which can be especially dangerous for people with weakened immune systems. The best alternative to tap water is to buy a water filter and attach it to your faucet at home. A wide variety of filters is available at many hardware and kitchen stores. When water is called for in

a smoothie recipe, we strongly recommend using filtered water.

Fruit juice and frozen juice concentrates. These are
excellent, easy ways to sweeten your smoothies naturally. Try to use all-natural varieties; you should
be able to find them in a natural food store if your
supermarket doesn't have them. When frozen juice
concentrates are called for, be careful not to use too
much, or the flavor will be too strong.

Ginseng powder. Ground ginseng root. It is often
used for medicinal purposes, and should only be
used in small quantities. It is available in bulk or
prepackaged at natural food stores.

Kelp. A sea vegetable that is usually sold in powdered form. It is high in protein, vitamins, and
amino acids, and is very flavorful; it is often used as
an alternative to salt. Kelp is available in bulk at
most natural food stores or groceries that specialize
in Japanese foods.

Milk (dairy). Any milk product that is derived from
an animal (such as a cow or goat). Dairy milk often
contains pesticides filtered through the animal's
system, as well as extremely high doses of calcium,
which the body has difficulty breaking down for
nutritional use. If dairy milk must be used, low-fat
or whole milk is preferred for taste.

Milk (non-dairy). Any non-animal milk product.
There is a wide variety on the market, including:
soy milk, which contains a high concentrate of protein; rice milk, which contains many essential
nutrients; and almond milk, which is also high in
protein. Almond milk, especially, can be used in

place of dairy for cereal, soups, or to drink straight. Like animal milk, non-dairy milk is available in a variety of flavors at natural food stores and in "natural food sections" at large chain supermarkets.

Mint syrup. A combination of mint, water, sugar, and corn syrup, that can be obtained at coffee houses or Italian delicatessens.

Miso. A combination of soybean powder, rice, and sea salt, used in soups and salad mixes, as well as smoothies. Unpasteurized white miso is preferred for these recipes. Miso can be obtained prepackaged at natural food stores and some supermarkets.

Pine nuts. Also known as pignoli, these are the edible seeds of a low-growing pine tree. They are a good source of protein and minerals, and are available in natural food stores and some supermarkets.

Protein powder. A combination of soy powder, lecithin, papain, and vanilla flavoring. This is available in bulk or prepackaged at natural food stores, vitamin centers, and some spas.

Spirulina. A form of algae high in protein, low in fat and cholesterol, and filled with vitamins, minerals, and other nutrients. It can be bought in liquid or powdered form, and flavored, at natural food stores, juice bars, and by mail order: Light Force, 1115 Thompson Avenue, #5, Santa Cruz, CA 95062, is one source.

Tahini. Sesame butter made from ground, hulled sesame seeds, in a thinner consistency than peanut butter. Tahini is mild and sweet, and a good source of protein. It is available at natural food stores and in the ethnic food section of some supermarkets.

Tofu. Pressed soybean curd. It is high in protein, and contains no cholesterol. It is available in soft or firm form. Tofu has no flavor of its own, but takes on that of other ingredients. It is an excellent meat substitute, and can be used like meat in every dish. It is packaged in a variety of formats at natural food stores and is obtainable in firm consistency at most major markets.

Wheat germ. The embryo of the wheat kernel, which contains nutrients galore, plus protein. Buy in bulk at natural food stores or in jars at major supermarkets. Wheat germ must be stored in the refrigerator.

Wheatgrass juice. Usually seven-day-old wheat plant sprouts that have been freshly juiced. Wheatgrass is high in vitamins A, B complex, and E, as well as minerals and chlorophyll; it is reported to have many medicinal benefits. It is available at natural food stores.

The Recipes*

1.
As Time Goes By

"As Time Goes By" is taken from the classic song of the same name in the movie *Casablanca*. It refers to our desire to find a true love that neither time nor distance can separate from our memories of romance, lost innocence, and new discovery. The chapter begins at daybreak and ends at the mid-night hour, with a corresponding smoothie to fill your needs every waking hour of the day.

Shona's Sun Salutation

This smoothie is one of our son Shona's favorites. It is good for small children, since the ice-cold water helps to relieve some of the pain of teething. It also gets your motor running in the morning. It has a good aftertaste and "tickles the mouth." Sunflower seeds are high in calcium and protein, while the raisins add just the right amount of sweetness.

Yield: 4 cups

2 cups ice-cold filtered water

2 large bananas

$3/4$ cup sunflower seeds

$3/4$ cup raisins

1. Place all the ingredients in a blender, and mix on medium speed for 2 minutes.

2. Pour into tall glasses and serve.

Morning Lift-Off

This contains a complete well-rounded breakfast for the athlete in each of us waiting to burst forth.

Yield: 5 cups

3 small bananas

2 cups fresh-squeezed orange juice

$1/2$ cup cooked oatmeal

$1/4$ cup Grape Nuts cereal*

$1/4$ cup firm tofu

1 tablespoon honey

1 egg, or $1 1/2$ teaspoons egg substitute plus 2 tablespoons water

1. Place all the ingredients in a blender, and mix on medium speed for 1 minute.

2. Pour into tall glasses and serve.

* In place of Grape Nuts, use brown rice cereal, oats, shredded wheat, or any other favorite grain cereal.

The Blue Dragon

Guaranteed to turn your tongue blue for the rest of the day. For a little fun, go see an acupuncturist immediately after drinking this smoothie. One of the first things they always do is look at your tongue to determine your state of health. They may think you're from Mars! Blueberries, by the way, are high in iron.

Yield: 4 cups

1 cup ripe, juicy blueberries

2 large bananas

2 cups watermelon juice

4 tablespoons plain yogurt

1/4 cup Grape Nuts cereal

1 tablespoon protein powder

1 1/2 teaspoons honey or brown rice syrup

1. Place all the ingredients in a blender, and mix on medium speed for 30 seconds.

2. Pour into tall glasses and serve.

Darci's Pineapple Delight

As our daughter Darci exclaims, "This breakfast drink is sweet, sweet, sweet. It fills my mouth with joy!" Pineapples are high in vitamin C and rich in potassium and calcium.

Yield: 4 cups

2 cups soy or rice milk

2 medium bananas

6 slices pineapple

4 tablespoons protein powder

1 tablespoon honey or brown rice syrup

1. Place all the ingredients in a blender, and mix on medium speed for 30 seconds.

2. Pour into tall glasses and serve.

Brown Sugar

This smoothie is great for breakfast or as a mid-morning pick-me-up. It provides you with lots of energy to face the day, and its sweetness will put a smile on your face!

Yield: 4^1/$_2$ cups

1 banana

2 cups filtered water

^{1}/$_3$ cup cooked oats

1 tablespoon plus 1^1/$_2$ teaspoons brown sugar

^{3}/$_4$ cup firm tofu

3 tablespoons plus 1^1/$_2$ teaspoons plain yogurt

1. Place all the ingredients in a blender, and blend on medium speed for 30 seconds.

2. Pour into tall glasses and serve.

KASHI®
KICK

Kashi® is a cereal mix of grains that provides protein beyond compare. It can be used in a variety of dishes, such as soups, salads, and smoothies, or as a hot cereal by itself.

You can buy Kashi already mixed, or you can make an equivalent yourself. Mix equal parts of barley, oats, millet, sesame seeds, and brown rice in a large pot with twice as much water as grain. Bring to a boil and simmer for about one hour. Use some for the next day or two, then freeze the remainder for use later on.

Yield: 4 cups

1 cup Kashi

2 cups milk (soy or dairy)

1 banana

1 tablespoon honey or brown rice syrup

1. Place all the ingredients in a blender, and mix on medium speed for 1 minute.

2. Pour into tall glasses and serve.

The
Milky Way

This is the perfect lunchtime smoothie. Make it at home and keep it in the refrigerator at work, or dash home during your break and make it then. The Milky Way will take you out of this world!

Yield: 4 cups

1 cup milk (dairy or non-dairy)
2 small ripe bananas
1 cup plain yogurt (dairy or non-dairy)
$1/2$ cup cottage cheese
(dairy or non-dairy)
2 tablespoons honey or brown rice syrup
$1/2$ cup fresh or frozen strawberries

1. Place all the ingredients in a blender, and mix on medium speed for 45 seconds.

2. Pour into tall glasses and serve.

The
Cowabunga

This is by far the surfing crowd's favorite party drink.

Yield: 5 cups

1 tablespoon chocolate syrup
3 tablespoons frozen orange juice
2 large ripe bananas
1 1/2 teaspoons peanut butter
1/2 cup filtered water
1 cup strawberry-lemonade juice*
1/2 teaspoon vanilla extract
1/2 cup firm tofu

1. Place all the ingredients in a blender, and mix on high speed for 30 seconds.

2. Pour into tall glasses and serve.

* Available commercially at natural food stores and some supermarket chains.

The CuGurt

Cucumbers are rich in magnesium, iron, and potassium, and are believed to assist the function of the liver and kidneys. The CuGurt is an excellent lunchtime meal.

Yield: 4 cups

2 cucumbers, peeled, seeded, and chopped
1 cup plain yogurt (soy or dairy)
2 tablespoons maple syrup
1 tablespoon lemon juice
2 tablespoons miso
2 mint leaves, finely chopped, or 1 tablespoon dried mint
1 cup filtered ice water
1/4 cup finely chopped walnuts

1. Place all the ingredients in a blender, and mix on medium speed for 1 minute.

2. Pour into tall glasses and serve.

THE SIESTA

Take a drink of The Siesta late in the afternoon, put on your sombrero, and snooze or watch the clouds drift by. Dream about the Smoothie Goddess or imagine yourself on the beach in Baja or Hawaii with nothing to do.

Yield: 4 cups

2 cups fresh seedless orange slices (about 1 1/2 - 2 oranges)

4 small ripe bananas

1/2 cup fresh or packaged coconut

1/2 cup unsalted peanuts

1/2 cup raspberry jam

1/4 cup wheat germ

1 cup filtered water

1. Place all the ingredients in a blender, and mix on high speed for 45 seconds.

2. Pour into tall glasses and serve.

A CUP OF
Zen

*The Buddha would gladly sit and drink this
enlightened cup of nirvana to attain eternal peace
and freedom from suffering. It's also nutritious,
filling, and simple. Dinner was never easier to make—
better than running out for pizza!*

Yield: 5 cups

$1/2$ cup cooked short grain brown rice

$2^1/2$ large ripe bananas

$1/2$ cup coconut milk

$1/2$ cup soy milk

$1/2$ cup firm tofu

$1/4$ cup wheat germ

$1/4$ cup chopped almonds

1. Place all the ingredients in a blender, and blend
on medium speed for 1 minute.

2. Pour into tall glasses and serve.

Sunset on the Water

Persimmons are rich in carbohydrates and potassium and have a wonderful blood-red color. Asian countries have grown them for years, although the United States now leads the world in production of these sugary fruits. This smoothie is the perfect accompaniment to sitting outside and watching the sun go down.

Yield: 4 cups

$1/2$ persimmon, peeled and seeded

1 tablespoon cinnamon

2 ripe bananas

$1/2$ cup raisins

2 cups filtered water

1 tablespoon brown rice syrup

1. Place all the ingredients in a blender, and blend on medium speed for 1 minute.

2. Pour into tall glasses and serve.

An Evening of Poetry

"I am giddy; expectation whirls me round.
Th' imaginary relish is so sweet, that it enchants
my sense." (From Shakespeare's The History of
Troilus and Cressida, *Act III, Scene ii). This*
smoothie is guaranteed to put you in a poetic mood.

Yield: 5 cups

10 Shakespearean strawberries

2 Poe pecans

2 large Browning bananas

1/4 cup sliced Angelou apple

1/2 cup Whitman water

1 cup ode orange juice

1 cup peeled and sliced Patrick papaya

1 cup Cary coconut-pineapple juice

1. Place all the ingredients in a blender, and blend on medium speed for 1 minute.

2. Pour into tall glasses and serve.

Poets to Drink With

Here are a few poets to share your smoothie with.

Edgar Allan Poe (1809–1849). Best known for short fiction and poems of horror.

William Shakespeare (1564–1616). Wrote the most influential body of literature by any individual in Western history. His work comprises thirty-six plays, one hundred fifty-four sonnets, and two narrative poems.

Walt Whitman (1819–1892). One of the greatest nineteenth-century American poets.

Alice Cary (1820–1871). She and her sister Phoebe wrote volumes of poems.

Robert Browning (1812–1889). One of the greatest Victorian poets.

Maya Angelou (born 1928). One of the greatest living American poets, playwrights, screen-writers, and composers.

Patrick Henry (1736–1799). American patriot, poet, and orator.

Burning the Midnight Oil

Guaranteed to give you an adrenaline rush and keep you awake to finish those last-minute projects or term papers due first thing in the morning. To live dangerously, substitute double espresso for the coffee, and prepare to stay up all night watching the late movies with a friend.

Yield: 4 cups

1/2 cup chocolate syrup

3 frozen bananas*

1 tablespoon protein powder

2 cups strong brewed coffee

1 tablespoon mint syrup

1 small brownie

1/2 teaspoon cinnamon

1. Place all the ingredients in a blender, and mix on medium speed for 1 minute.

2. Pour into tall glasses and serve.

* To make frozen bananas, peel and chop the bananas, seal in plastic bags, and place in the freezer until frozen.

2.
A Smoothie for All Seasons

One of the most important aspects of any holiday is the food. Just think of Thanksgiving without the meal! Here's a chance to celebrate the holidays in style. Instead of the usual fare, try a unique smoothie to complement your Thanksgiving dinner, Halloween party, New Year's celebration, or any other special occasion. If you can't wait until the next holiday, invent your own and celebrate with a smoothie for all seasons.

Eggnog Fog

Eggnog, originally from Great Britain, is now a favorite winter drink for the holidays throughout much of the world. It has a distinct taste that one either loves or hates.

Yield: 4 cups

3 cups eggnog

1 tablespoon nutmeg

1 tablespoon cinnamon

1 banana

2 tablespoons maple syrup

1. Place all the ingredients in a blender, and mix on medium speed for 30 seconds.

2. Pour into tall glasses and serve.

EL TOMATE CALIENTE
[The Hot Tomato]

Celebrate Cinco de Mayo (Mexican independence day) with The Hot Tomato every May fifth, or any other time of the year you wish to declare your independence. This is a hot, hot smoothie guaranteed to set your throat on fire.

Yield: 4 cups

2 cups tomato juice

1/2 small jalapeño pepper, chopped*

2 pinches cayenne pepper

2 slices onion, chopped (about 1/4 cup)

2 pinches parsley

2 teaspoons garlic powder

1. Place all the ingredients in a blender, and mix on high speed for 30 seconds. Throw in some tortilla chips at your discretion.

2. Pour into tall glasses and serve.

---

*Jalapeño and other hot peppers must be handled carefully. You should especially avoid contact with the seeds. Use a fork to hold the pepper while chopping. Wash your hands when you are finished, and do not put your fingers in your eyes or near your face.

Spice of Life

"They" say variety is the spice of life. This holiday drink has all the colors of falling leaves and a perfect blend of sweetness and spice to get you in the spirit. Dates, originally from the Middle East, are a good source of energy and a great sweet to use instead of candy.

Yield: 5 cups

1/4 teaspoon cinnamon

3 dates, pitted and chopped

1/2 cup roasted cashews

3/4 teaspoon ground cloves

3/4 cup firm tofu

1/2 cup plain yogurt

3 cups apple juice

1. Place all the ingredients in a blender, and blend on high speed for 45 seconds.

2. Pour into tall glasses and serve.

Audrey's Amore

If there is indeed a true aphrodisiac, this is it. Chocolate and strawberries—what a treat for Valentine's Day! For a truly romantic and adventurous experience, drink one smoothie out of a single glass together with two straws, then take another full glass, slowly pour it over each other's naked bodies, and do as you wish. (Be prepared to take a warm bubble bath immediately afterwards, or you'll stick to your sheets and clothes for days.)

Yield: 5 cups

3 cups chocolate milk (dairy, soy, or rice)

10 large ripe strawberries

2 small bananas

2 tablespoons cocoa powder

2 tablespoons finely chopped fresh mint

1. Place all the ingredients in a blender, and blend on medium speed for 1 minute.

2. Pour into tall glasses and serve.

THE
GREAT PUMPKIN

This smoothie tastes just like pumpkin pie á la mode; it's great for Thanksgiving, or any other winter holdiay. Pumpkins are a good source of fiber, and are rich in vitamin A and silicon.

Yield: $4^1/2$ cups

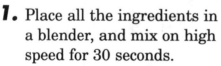

$3/4$ cup canned pumpkin

$3/4$ teaspoon nutmeg

3 cups soy milk

$3/4$ teaspoon cinnamon

$3/4$ teaspoon vanilla extract

$1^1/2$ cups vanilla ice cream

1. Place all the ingredients in a blender, and mix on high speed for 30 seconds.

2. Pour into tall glasses and serve.

JERRY'S
Sweet Potato

In addition to being one of Grandpa Jerry's favorite recipes for Thanksgiving, sweet potatoes are very rich in niacin. And Grandpa's not the only lover of sweet potato!

Yield: 4$\frac{1}{2}$ cups

1 cup chopped, cooked sweet potato*

2 cups orange juice

1 banana

$\frac{1}{2}$ cup marshmallows

$\frac{1}{2}$ cup light brown sugar

1. Place all the ingredients in a blender, and blend on medium speed for 1 minute.

2. Pour into tall glasses and serve.

*Bake sweet potatoes at 400°F for 40 minutes, or until soft.

The Tingler

For your next New Year's Eve or Winter Solstice celebration, make a resolution with this bubbly, non-alcoholic crowd-pleaser.

Yield: 5 cups

$1/4$ cup filtered cold water

$3/4$ cup boysenberry juice

$1/2$ cup frozen orange juice concentrate

3 small bananas

$1/4$ cup firm tofu

8 fresh strawberries

$1/4$ cup plain yogurt

$1/4$ cup cashews

1 cup sparkling mineral water

1. Place all the ingredients, except the mineral water, in a blender, and mix on medium speed for 1 minute.

2. Add the mineral water, and blend on low speed for 5 seconds.

3. Pour into tall glasses and serve.

3.
Travel the Seven Seas

Smoothie ingredients come from all corners of the planet—Asia, South America, Africa, Europe, North America, and the South Sea Islands. Smoothies are a cross-cultural experience of diversity and harmony mixed in a single glass. Stop and think about your friends and neighbors around the globe while enjoying these drinks. Smoothies won't put an end to hatred, racism, and war—but then again, who knows?

Down Under

The raspberry hits you strongly at first, then a nice aftertaste of kiwi and almond kicks in to finish it off. Kiwis, identified worldwide with New Zealand, are high in vitamin C. They help maintain healthy gums and teeth, as well as aid in digestion.

Yield: 4 cups

2 ripe kiwis, peeled and sliced

2 tablespoons plain yogurt

1 ripe banana

1 cup raspberry juice

1 tablespoon almond butter

1. Place all the ingredients in a blender, and mix on medium speed for 30 seconds.

2. Pour into tall glasses and serve.

LAND OF THE
Buddha

Buddhism first spread throughout Asia from India into Burma, Cambodia, China, Laos, Sri Lanka, Tibet, and Japan. Gautama Buddha once said, "Desire is a trap. Desirelessness is liberation." Obviously he had never tasted a smoothie, or he would have said, "Desire is freedom, and the best desire of all is for smoothies." Over the last few years, many Buddhists have been known to be secretly converting to Smoothism. This is a simple, satisfying meal, which, like Buddhism, is nourishing and easy to digest.

Yield: 5 cups

$1/2$ cup filtered water

1 cup coconut milk

1 banana

$1/2$ cup shelled, unsalted peanuts

$1/2$ cup cooked rice

$1/2$ pineapple, peeled and chopped

1. Place all the ingredients in a blender, and blend on low speed for 45 seconds.

2. Pour into tall glasses and serve.

Luscious Lassi

Lassi is an Indian drink made with dairy, honey, and fruit. In India, you'll often see people greet one another by putting their palms together and saying, "Namaste" ("I honor the light within you"). The Luscious Lassi is a cool, refreshing smoothie which honors the light within each one of us. One sip and you'll think you're in Kashmir, in Northern India, at the foot of the Himalayas.

Yield: $4^1/2$ cups

3 tablespoons plain yogurt

$1^1/2$ ripe mangoes, peeled, seeded, and sliced

3 cups milk (soy or dairy)

3 tablespoons honey

1. Place all the ingredients in a blender, and blend on low speed for 1 minute.

2. Pour into tall glasses and serve.

ALMOND LASSI

Another variation of a cool Indian refresher.

Yield: 3 cups

1 cup almond milk, chilled

2 dates, chopped

$1/2$ teaspoon ground cardamom

$1/4$ teaspoon ground black pepper

1. Place all the ingredients in a blender, and blend on medium speed for 30 seconds.

2. Pour into tall glasses and serve.

THE MAHATMA

Mahatma Gandhi was one of India's most celebrated citizens. He practiced and advocated nonviolence, and helped India gain its independence from the British in 1947. As a strict vegetarian and a proponent of living simply, his primary diet consisted of rice, as does that of most Indians. This is a tasty smoothie, better than the best Indian restaurant in town.

Yield: $4^1/2$ cups

$3/4$ teaspoon curry powder

$3/4$ cup raisins

$3/4$ cup chopped cashews

$3/4$ cup plain yogurt

3 cups milk (soy or rice)

$1^1/2$ cups cooked short grain brown rice

1. Place all the ingredients in a blender, and mix on medium speed for 1 minute or longer, until desired texture (smooth or creamy) is reached.

2. Pour into tall glasses and serve.

LETI'S CHAI

This smoothie is one of my daughter Leti's favorites. Chai is a traditional Indian spiced tea made with cinnamon, nutmeg, ginger, cloves, dates, and cardamom. It can be bought prepackaged, or you can make it yourself (see page 14 for more information).

Yield: 3 cups

2 cups chai, steeped and cooled

1/2 cup rice milk

1 tablespoon honey, or to taste

1 tablespoon dried mint

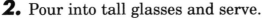

1. Place all the ingredients in a blender, and mix on medium speed for 1 minute.

2. Pour into tall glasses and serve.

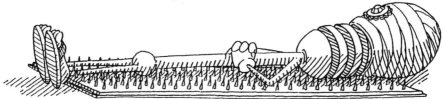

The Tex-Mex

Jicama is a root vegetable similar to the turnip. It is popular in Mexican dishes throughout Mexico, Texas, California, and New Mexico. This smoothie is sweet, hot, nourishing, and filling.

Yield: 5 cups

2 cups chopped fresh pineapple

1 small jicama, peeled and sliced

1 large mango, peeled and sliced

1 teaspoon chopped jalapeño pepper*

Juice of 1 lime

2 cups filtered water

1 banana

1. Place all the ingredients in a blender, and blend on high speed for 1 minute.

2. Pour into tall glasses and serve.

*Jalapeño and other hot peppers must be handled carefully. See page 39 for instructions.

Figaro, Figaro, Figaro!!!

The fig's praises have been sung for centuries. It is used extensively in the Mediterranean and the Middle East in a variety of dishes. It is also a surefire laxative when needed. You are encouraged to sing while making this smoothie. Pretend you're Placido Domingo or Luciano Pavarotti performing at the Metropolitan Opera in New York City, or in the shower.

Yield: 3 cups

4 baked figs*

1/2 cup cooked raisins**

1/2 cup chopped walnuts

1/2 cup plain yogurt

1 cup filtered water

1. Place all the ingredients in a blender, and mix on medium speed for 1 minute. Don't forget to sing!

2. Pour into tall glasses and serve.

* Bake figs at 350°F for 10 minutes.
** Place raisins in a saucepan with enough water to cover, bring to a boil, and simmer for 5 minutes.

RASPBERRY

Razzle Dazzle

This is a favorite and legendary thirst-quencher from Wisconsin in the 1960s and 1970s. Folks used to drive long distances to obtain this sweet, fresh drink. Raspberries are reported to help cleanse the body of toxins, and also contain vitamins C and A.

Yield: 4 cups

1 cup fresh raspberries

2 cups vanilla pudding

$1/2$ cup chopped pecans

1 cup filtered water

1. Place all the ingredients in a blender, and mix on medium speed for 50 to 60 seconds.

2. Pour into tall glasses and serve.

AGUA ARROZ

Agua arroz (rice water) is a favorite for breakfast in Mexico. Instead of throwing out the water used to cook rice for dinner, let the water soak overnight with cooked rice, and use it in the morning for your smoothie.

Yield: 3 cups

1 1/2 cups rice water

1 cup coconut milk

1 teaspoon cinnamon

1 tablespoon brown rice syrup

1. Place all the ingredients in a blender, and mix on medium speed for 30 seconds.

2. Pour into tall glasses and serve.

Bird of Paradise

To thoroughly enjoy this smoothie, take off your shirt, throw on a flower garland necklace, start dancing the hula, and let your mind drift off to a warm night in Tahiti.

Yield: 5 cups

1/2 cup fresh, shredded coconut

2 cups filtered water

3 large bananas

1/2 mango, peeled and chopped

1/2 papaya, peeled and chopped

1/4 passion fruit, peeled and chopped

1/2 guava, peeled and chopped

1 small slice pineapple

1. Place all the ingredients in a blender, and blend on high speed for 30 seconds. Include shaved ice for sweltering days.

2. Pour into tall glasses and serve.

4.
Kick Up Your Heels

Dance, dance, dance, for exercise, fun, or romance! Dances reflect your mood and your feelings, and bring energy and joy to your life. We're born to move. Dancing works up a good sweat and is the perfect excuse (as if you need one!) to have a drink to cool down. And what better drink is there than a refreshing smoothie? Wiggle through this chapter with your own rhythm and pace. If you're not already dancing, choose a style that suits you and find a local class, an instructor, or a friend. Have a great time!

Twist & Shout

The Twist was a popular dance, and a song by Chubby Checker, that swept the nation in the early 1960s. You put one foot in front of the other and twist your body from side to side, lifting one foot at a time for emphasis and bending your knees up and down. When you're finished doing the Twist, try this smoothie—it'll give you something to shout about.

Yield: 4 cups

2 tablespoons sunflower seeds

2 cups almond milk

2 dates, chopped

2 bananas

6 teaspoons carob powder

2 teaspoons vanilla extract

1. Place all the ingredients in a blender, and mix on medium speed for 45 seconds.

2. Pour into tall glasses and serve.

Strawberry
S T R U T

Clasp this drink in your hand and truck on down to your favorite hot spot to "strut your stuff." With the added oxygen your body receives from the strawberries, you'll have all the extra energy you need.

Yield: 4 cups

2 cups almond milk

20 fresh, ripe strawberries

1 small European or Japanese plum

2 teaspoons vanilla extract

2 pecans, chopped

2 tablespoons honey

1. Place all the ingredients in a blender, and mix on medium speed for 30 seconds.

2. Pour into tall glasses and serve.

Tango with the Mango

It is believed the tango is a dance that originally derived from the milonga of Argentina and the habanera of Cuba and the West Indies. It became popular in the United States and Europe around World War I. It is a flowing, elegant combination of movements accompanied by romantic, lively music with a throbbing beat.

There are hundreds of varieties of the delicious mango, including red, green, yellow, and orange. Mangoes are reported to help rid the body of unwanted odors, and to reduce fevers. They are high in vitamin A, and are said to delay some effects of aging if they are eaten frequently.

Yield: 5 cups

1 ripe mango, peeled and seeded

$1/2$ cup pomegranate juice

1 tangerine, peeled, seeded, and sliced

1 banana

1 ripe papaya, peeled, seeded, and sliced

2 cups filtered water

1. Place all the ingredients in a blender, and blend on medium speed for 45 seconds.

2. Pour into tall glasses and serve.

CANTALOUPE
WALTZ

The waltz is a gliding, turning dance that overcame hostile opposition to dominate social dancing from 1750 to 1900. It involves six even steps and full turns as slowly or swiftly as the music will take you. Famous early proponents were Johann Strauss and Josef Lanner.

Cantaloupes are said to alleviate some allergies, reduce bladder infections, relieve bursitis, and prevent memory loss.

Yield: 5 cups

$1/2$ cantaloupe, peeled, seeded, and sliced

$1/2$ honeydew, peeled, seeded, and sliced

2 cups filtered ice water

$1 1/2$ fresh mint leaves, finely chopped, or
1 tablespoon dried mint

8 ice cubes

3 teaspoons lime juice

1 teaspoon sea salt

10 fresh strawberries

1. Place all the ingredients in a blender, and mix on medium speed for 1 minute.

2. Pour into tall glasses and serve.

All That Jazz

Jazz is an original art form of American music that first became popular in the 1920s. It has continued to expand and deepen its roots throughout the music world. Elements of jazz have been integrated into classical, folk, blues, soul, country, rock, and rap music. Duke Ellington, Miles Davis, Chick Corea, Dizzy Gillespie, Thelonious Monk, Dave Brubeck, and John Coltrane are just a few of its famous innovators. This smoothie is perfect to drink while listening to their music—or at any other time, of course.

Yield: $4^1/2$ cups

$2^1/2$ medium bananas

3 tablespoons brewer's yeast

$1^1/2$ teaspoons cinnamon

$2^1/2$ cups apple juice

3 apricots, finely chopped

3 tablespoons honey

1. Place all the ingredients in a blender, and blend on medium speed for 1 minute.

2. Pour into tall glasses and serve.

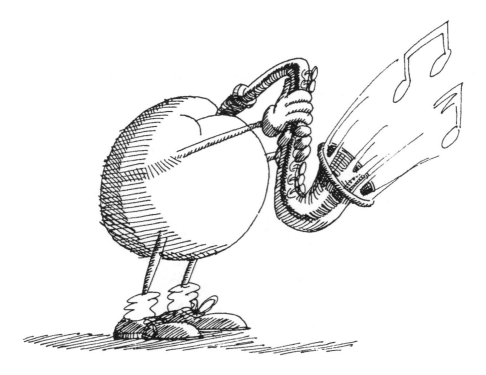

Charleston Cherry

The Charleston was the ballroom sensation of the 1920s. Named for Charleston, South Carolina, it is believed to have evolved from African-American dance steps then common, called the Jay-Bird and the Juba. It began simply as a rhythmic twisting of the feet, but when it reached Harlem it took on a fast, flapping kick. In 1923, a revue called Runnin' Wild was presented in New York City by Cecil Mack and James P. Johnson; it featured the Charleston and ignited the public's demand for this dance throughout the land.

You'll enjoy this cool Southern thirst-quencher any time of the year.

Yield: 4^1/$_2$ cups

^{1}/$_2$ cup plain yogurt

^{1}/$_2$ frozen banana (see page 36)

20 pitted cherries

1 ripe banana

2 cups filtered water

1. Place all the ingredients in a blender, and blend on high speed for 30 seconds.

2. Pour into tall glasses and serve.

Blueberry Boogie

Boogie Woogie is another American original. It is a spin-off of jazz and rhythm and blues that influenced rock-and-roll. One person who helped popularize this style was Fats Domino, whose song "Blueberry Hill," was a big seller. "Fats" was so named because of his large size—when he sat on the piano bench, it would disappear from view.

Drink the Blueberry Boogie when you've got the blues. It will lift your spirits and your blood sugar.

Yield: 4 cups

1 cup soft tofu

2 cups frozen blueberries

2 tablespoons honey

5 drops peppermint extract

2 cups filtered water

1. Place all the ingredients in a blender, and mix on high speed for 30 seconds.

2. Pour into tall glasses and serve.

5.
Healing Waters

The famous Greek physician Hippocrates (circa 431 B.C.) once said, "Let thy food be thy medicine." He would have loved smoothies! I can think of nothing better for your body than a smoothie filled with vitamins, minerals, carbohydrates, and protein to enhance your natural healing processes. There are some people who claim that various foods (vegetables, fruits, herbs, juices, etc.) can cure or prevent everything under the sun from cancer and AIDS to diabetes, strokes, heart attacks, and common colds. We don't have any intention of making such claims. Smoothies are not the cure-all to end all, but there are many individuals who believe smoothies have contributed to their well-being and recovery from illness, increased their energy, and restored their vitality. In addition to their healthy qualities, of course, smoothies also taste terrific, and the smoothies in this chapter are no exception.

Mellow Fellow

Calm that tummy. Get rid of indigestion. Quiet the baby. Peppermint provides energy, relaxation, and calmness.

Yield: 3 1/2 cups

1 cup brewed peppermint tea

2 fresh parsley leaves, chopped, or 1 table-spoon dried parsley

1 cup coconut milk

1 cup carrot juice

4 tablespoons maple syrup

1. Place all the ingredients in a blender, and mix on medium speed for 30 seconds.

2. Pour into tall glasses and serve.

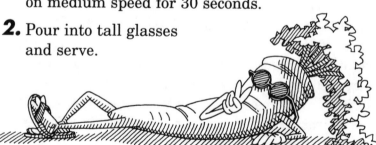

SMOOTH MOVE

*Grapefruit is low in calories and high in vitamins
B_1, B_2, and C. It also prevents constipation and
helps you sleep soundly, so this smoothie makes
a great bedtime snack.*

Yield: 3 cups

1 cup grapefruit juice

1 $^1/_2$ ripe bananas

1 prune, chopped

1 apricot, chopped

3 tablespoons honey

1. Place all the ingredients in a blender, and mix
on medium speed for 1 minute.

2. Pour into tall glasses
and serve.

Flower power

*Deja vu! This is a beautiful, colorful, nostalgic
drink, brimming with healthy ingredients.
Dandelion greens are a great diuretic; chamomile
is a relaxant; red clover blossom is a blood purifier;
and sage relieves sore throats. These can be found in
some natural food stores, or in your garden or fields.
This smoothie was inspired by the "flower children"
of the 1960s, who congregated in San Francisco
and preached a lifestyle of peace and love. Burning
incense and wearing a peace symbol and flowers in
your hair while making this smoothie are optional.*

Yield: 4 cups

2 cups milk (dairy or non-dairy)

4 tablespoons honey or brown rice syrup

2 tablespoons flower petals from nasturtium,
dandelion greens, chamomile, red clover
blossom, sage, and rose petal, as available

4 tablespoons vanilla ice cream

2 mint leaves, chopped, or 1 tablespoon
dried mint

1. Place all the ingredients in a blender, and mix on medium speed for 1 minute.

2. Pour into tall glasses and serve.

Purple People Pleaser

The color of this drink is a sight to see, and it tastes like velvet-smooth grapes caressing your taste buds. The pineapple juice helps reduce weight by digesting proteins, and the bananas provide potassium.

Yield: 4 cups

6 tablespoons frozen
grape juice concentrate

1 slice fresh pineapple

1 cup filtered water

1 banana

1 tablespoon almond butter

1 tablespoon maple syrup

1. Place all the ingredients in a blender, and blend on medium speed for 30 seconds.

2. Pour into tall glasses and serve.

Wheatgrass Wonder

Wheatgrass juice helps cleanse the body of toxins, purifies the liver, and reportedly helps damaged cells heal. Reactions to the Wheatgrass Wonder range from "shock" and "fabulous" to "stimulating" and "arousing."

Yield: 4 cups

$^1/_2$ cup wheatgrass juice

1 cup fresh-squeezed orange juice

4 tablespoons lime juice

12 ice cubes, crushed

1. Place all the ingredients in a blender, and blend on high speed for 30 seconds.

2. Pour into tall glasses and serve.

Hospice Healer

Hospices originally began in Europe as places of rest for the Crusaders. They evolved over the centuries into a unique program to provide care for those facing life-threatening illness. In recent years, hospices have spread throughout Europe and the United States. They provide symptom control and relief from pain, as well as psychosocial and spiritual support for both the patients and their families.

The Hospice Healer is easy to drink. Like all smoothies, it is ideal for those on soft diets. It provides protein and calories to maintain weight, and is invaluable when convalescing or chronically ill. It can be drunk throughout the day.

Yield: 4^1/$_2$ cups

2 cups rice milk

2 cups your favorite berries

^{1}/$_2$ teaspoon spirulina

^{1}/$_2$ teaspoon protein powder

1^1/$_2$ cups soft tofu

2 ripe bananas

4 multivitamins, crushed

1. Place all the ingredients in a blender, and mix on medium speed for 1 minute.

2. Pour into tall glasses and serve.

Cold
COMFORT

Garlic is truly the patient's best friend. It helps cleanse the throat, sinuses, nose, and lungs. It has been used to ward off werewolves, vampires, and "the evil eye," and has been praised as a cure for every calamity imaginable. Some people believe that if you eat or drink enough garlic, you will live forever. Of course, you may live alone, due to its strong smell.

Yield: 3 cups

1/2 teaspoon garlic powder

Pinch cayenne pepper

1/2 teaspoon ground ginger

3 ripe bananas

2 cups apple juice

2 teaspoons maple syrup

1/4 cup firm tofu

1. Place all the ingredients in a blender, and mix on medium speed for 30 seconds.

2. Pour into tall glasses and serve. Drink in small amounts.

NEIGHBORHOOD NECTAR

Ah, nectarines! What a treat. Not only do they taste fabulous, but they are also rich in potassium, sodium, and calcium. Nectarines help clean out the toxic crud that accumulates in your pores, thus aiding your complexion. Try sharing this smoothie with your neighbors—they'll love it!

Yield: 5 cups

6 tablespoons plain yogurt (soy or dairy)

6 fresh nectarines, peeled and sliced

1 1/2 tablespoons honey, or to taste

1/3 cup wheat germ

1 cup seedless grapes

3 cups filtered water

1. Place all the ingredients in a blender, and blend on medium speed for 45 seconds.

2. Pour into tall glasses and serve.

Tahini Genie

Tahini is sesame butter. It can also be used for salads, dips, and sauces, and provides a creamy, rich, nutty taste. Sesame seeds are an excellent source of many nutrients, including calcium, phosphorus, lecithin, and amino acids.

Yield: 4 cups

2 cups filtered cold water

2 frozen bananas (see page 36)

1 tablespoon plus ³/₄ teaspoon tahini

1 teaspoon vanilla

1. Place all the ingredients in a blender, and mix on high speed for 30 seconds.

2. Pour into tall glasses and serve.

GODZILLA'S GINSENG

Ginseng is known throughout the world as a powerful tonic and energizer. It's prescribed in China for ailments ranging from colds to impotence. You can use it in stir fry, salads, drinks, soups, and healing remedies, such as this natural breath freshener. It has a zingy taste that, like Godzilla, lasts forever.

Yield: 3 cups

3 tablespoons powdered ginseng

3 tablespoons fresh lemon juice

3 tablespoons fresh lime juice

3 fresh mint leaves, chopped

1 $1/2$ cups filtered water

1 tablespoon plus 1 $1/2$ teaspoons
maple syrup

1. Place all the ingredients in a blender, and mix on medium speed for 30 seconds.

2. Chill the mixture in the freezer for 15 minutes.

3. Pour into tall glasses and serve with a slice of lemon or lime on top.

THE
ℬETA-ℭAROTENE ℚUEEN

*"It sure is orange!" That's what most people say
when they see this smoothie for the first time.
Do not look directly at this drink without the aid
of sunglasses, or it may cause blindness. This is a
tangy, sweet drink fit for royalty. It's healthy, too.
The apricots provide a high sugar content for energy;
the carrot juice is high in vitamin A; the orange
juice is high in vitamin C; cantaloupe aids in
elimination; mango helps reduce fever; and papaya
is rich in vitamins. Save the peels from the fruit
and use for cups.*

Yield: 4 cups

2 apricots, pitted and sliced

1 1/2 cups carrot juice

1/2 cup peeled and chopped cantaloupe

1/2 cup peeled and sliced mango

1 cup peeled and chopped papaya

3 tablespoons frozen orange juice concentrate,
or 1 cup fresh orange juice

1. Place all the ingredients in a blender, and blend on low speed for 1 minute.

2. Pour into tall glasses and serve.

Grandma Grandy's Cranberry
CRUNCH

This smoothie is not for the faint of heart; it is a sweet and tart elixir with a very strong flavor. Cranberry juice is excellent for relief of urinary tract and yeast infections. Make sure you use 100 percent pure cranberry juice, not the watered-down cranberry blends often sold in supermarkets.

Yield: 5 cups

2$\frac{1}{2}$ cups pure cranberry juice

2 tablespoons frozen lemonade concentrate,
or 2 cups fresh lemonade

1 cup apple juice

2 ripe bananas

1 cup seedless grapes

$\frac{3}{4}$ cup Grape Nuts cereal

$\frac{3}{4}$ cup honey

1. Place all the ingredients in a blender, and purée on medium speed for 1 minute.

2. Pour into tall glasses and serve.

C A P C T A I N

This will knock out those nasty cold bugs in no time flat. The oranges, tangerine, lemon, grapefruit, and lime all contain high amounts of vitamin C. The bananas give this smoothie some body, and the honey and strawberries provide sweetness.

Yield: 5 cups

2 cups filtered water

2 large sweet oranges, peeled and sliced

2 large ripe bananas

1 small tangerine, peeled and sliced

$1/4$ small lemon, peeled and sliced

$1/4$ small grapefruit, peeled and sliced

$1/2$ medium lime, peeled and sliced

4 tablespoons honey

8 large fresh strawberries

1. Place all the ingredients in a blender, and blend on medium speed for 45 seconds.

2. Pour into tall glasses and serve.

That Old Black Magic

Spirulina is a form of algae. It's a big energy booster that the Aztecs used to take on long trips. Rose hip tea is high in vitamin C, and helps fight off colds. This smoothie should be dark in color.

Yield: 4 cups

1/4 cup spirulina

1 large banana

1/2 cup plain yogurt

1 cup grape juice

1/4 cup lemon juice

2 tablespoons honey

1/2 cup brewed rose hip tea

1. Place all the ingredients in a blender, and mix on medium speed for 30 seconds.

2. Pour into tall glasses and serve.

On Cloud
NINE

This is a healthy dessert drink full of protein, vitamins, and taste. It will put you into the clouds!

Yield: 5 cups

4 small ripe bananas

$2^1/_2$ cups filtered water

1 8-ounce can frozen orange juice concentrate

$^1/_4$ cup firm tofu

$^1/_4$ cup protein powder

3 heaping tablespoons powdered chocolate or strawberry spirulina

1. Place all the ingredients in a blender, and mix on medium speed for 1 minute.

2. Pour into tall glasses and serve.

The Green
Turtle

This "totally green" drink is one of Kermit the Frog's favorites. It is also well liked by Mutant Ninjas, Mr. Greenjeans, and the '60s rock group, The Turtles. Soy milk is high in protein. Kelp is filled with iodine and, in small quantities, is reported to decrease negative thyroid conditions.

Yield: 5 cups

3 large kiwis, peeled and sliced
2 large ripe bananas
$^1/_2$ cup plain yogurt
1 $^1/_2$ cups filtered water
$^1/_4$ teaspoon almond extract
1 cup seedless grapes
$^1/_2$ cup soy milk
1 tablespoon kelp
3 tablespoons honey

1. Place all the ingredients in a blender, and blend on medium speed for 1 minute.

2. Pour into tall glasses and serve.

Completely
NUTZ

You'll feel a little nutty after you swig down this concoction loaded with minerals, protein, and iron.

Yield: 5 cups

2 large ripe bananas

2 cups filtered water

1 tablespoon peanut butter

1 cup orange juice

1 cup fruit punch

1 tablespoon honey

1/4 cup chopped pecans, cashews,
or walnuts

1/4 cup pine (or pignoli) nuts

1. Place all the ingredients in a blender, and mix on medium speed for 1 1/2 minutes.

2. Pour into tall glasses and serve.

6.
For Adults Only

Alcoholic beverages have a long history. When used habitually or in excess, they can cause serious physical and mental damage. When consumed in moderation, they can enhance a party, dinner, or special event by decreasing chemical inhibitors and increasing the "happy" buttons in the brain. You may know of other drinks that have this effect, but none are as unique or tasty as the smoothies in this chapter. Remember not to drive after drinking the following smoothies. If you like, you may omit the alcohol from these recipes and enjoy them as non-alcoholic thirst quenchers.

The Atom Smasher

Guaranteed to clear up your sinuses, wake up your taste buds, and send a shiver up your spine.

Yield: 2¹/₂ cups, or 6 shot-glasses full

1 cup vegetable juice (such as V-8 or another variety)

2 or 3 tablespoons vodka

¹/₈ teaspoon Tabasco hot pepper sauce

Pinch cayenne pepper

¹/₄ teaspoon pepper

¹/₄ teaspoon salt

1. Place all the ingredients in a blender, and stir on low speed for 30 seconds.

2. Pour into tall glasses and serve.

Piña Colada
GOT YA

A cool refresher. If you're cuckoo for coconut, then this is your dream smoothie.

Yield: 3 cups

$3/4$ cup coconut milk

2 slices fresh pineapple, chopped (about $1/2$ cup)

1 small banana

$3/4$ cup vanilla-flavored soy milk

$1/2$ apple, peeled, seeded, and sliced

4 tablespoons rum

1. Place all the ingredients in a blender, and blend on medium speed for 45 seconds.

2. Pour into tall glasses and serve.

KINKY KAHLÚA

If you love Kahlúa, drink this smoothie and you'll fly straight to heaven.

Yield: 4 servings

2 cups milk (dairy, soy, or rice)

4 tablespoons chocolate syrup

20 fresh strawberries

$^1/_2$ cup Kahlúa coffee liqueur

1. Place all the ingredients in a blender, and blend on medium speed for 1 minute.

2. Pour into tall glasses and serve.

BOTTOMS UP

This smoothie is frothy, delicious, and calming.
It's especially good if you can't fall asleep at night.

Yield: 3 cups

2 cups rice milk

2 tablespoons brewed chamomile tea

2 small bananas

$1/4$ cup brandy

2 tablespoons maple syrup

1. Place all the ingredients in a blender, and purée on low speed for 30 seconds.

2. Pour into tall glasses and serve.

DYNAMITE DAIQUIRI

The reviews are in. Critics across the country agree about this smoothie. "Very good!" "Goes well with dinner." "I give it four stars." "Two thumbs up." "Drink it with a friend." This is a high-powered drink, not for the faint of heart.

Yield: 4 cups

$1/2$ cup tequila

2 teaspoons lime juice

$1/2$ cup crushed ice

16 frozen strawberries

2 bananas

1 cup lemonade

1. Place all the ingredients in a blender, and blend on medium speed for 1 minute.

2. Pour into tall glasses and serve.

7.
Declassified

This was a difficult array of recipes to obtain. I had to use all the skills I've learned from my training with the X-Files, Get Smart, James Bond, and countless hours in the battlefield of parenthood. I bring these cloak-and-dagger drinks to your attention with a price on my head, but I had no choice. I couldn't live with myself if these remained a mystery; the guilt would have been overwhelming.

The
$\mathscr{S}$*ensuous*
Safari

This smoothie has been used to entice foreign heads of state to reveal their nation's most intimate secrets. When given a choice between The Sensuous Safari or money, nine out of ten dignitaries chose The Safari.

Yield: 4$^1/_2$ cups

1 cup peach nectar

1 cup boysenberry nectar

2 slices fresh pineapple

1 mango, peeled and sliced

2 bananas

1. Place all the ingredients in a blender, and blend on medium speed for 30 seconds.

2. Pour into tall glasses and serve.

Brendon's Blueberry Sparkle

This is a nice dinner drink to top off the evening after a long day of intrigue. This formula has been tested as a truth serum on unknowing CIA agents for thirty years. The results were unexpected; the agents had to tell the truth, and they all loved it. It's one of my son Brendon's favorites, too.

Yield: 5 cups

1 cup fresh blueberries

1 cup seedless grapes

$1/4$ teaspoon ground ginger

2 cups sparkling water

1. Place the berries, grapes, and ground ginger in a blender, and blend on medium speed for one minute.

2. Add the sparkling water, and blend on low speed for 5 seconds.

3. Pour into tall glasses and serve.

The Picasso

As Picasso's paintings fill your eyes with images of color, this smoothie will fill your mouth with an array of flavors and inundate your taste buds with a splash of brilliance. I had to travel by time machine to meet Picasso in person and obtain this recipe from his private diary.

Yield: 5 cups

1 cup filtered water

2 large bananas

1/2 cup raspberries

6-10 seedless grapes

1/4 cup Grape-Nuts cereal

1/2 cup frozen orange juice concentrate

1/4 cup cranberry juice

1/4 cup firm tofu

1 tablespoon protein powder

1 teaspoon peanut butter

1 tablespoon ground ginger

1 tablespoon honey

1 teaspoon vanilla extract

1. Place all the ingredients in a blender, and blend on high speed for 1 minute.

2. Pour into tall glasses and serve.

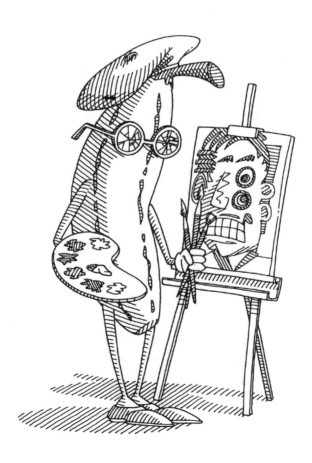

The Voluptuous Violet

Lady Godiva had nothing on The Voluptuous Violet. Its captivating taste surpasses the alluring talents of even Cleopatra and Mata Hari. The Voluptuous Violet was kept from the public for many years for fear it would create emotional dependence and turn ordinary citizens into Madonna clones.

Yield: 5 cups

$1/4$ cup seedless grapes

$1/4$ cup blueberries

$1/2$ cup applesauce

3 cups filtered water

1 large banana

$1/4$ cup firm tofu

1 teaspoon vanilla extract

1 tablespoon honey

1. Place all the ingredients in a blender, and blend on medium speed for 30 seconds.

2. Pour into tall glasses and serve.

THE
Unthinkable

The recipe for The Unthinkable was classified as TOP SECRET by the U.S. Government for the last fifty years, but it has now been smuggled out of the Pentagon for your personal enjoyment. Make sure the lights are off and the blinds are drawn when you concoct this classified secret smoothie.

Yield: 5 cups

2 cups filtered water

1 cup frozen orange juice concentrate

1 large nectarine, peeled and sliced

2 frozen bananas (see page 36)

1 tablespoon honey

1 cup kiwi-strawberry juice

1. Place all the ingredients in a blender, and blend on medium speed for 30 seconds.

2. Pour into tall glasses and serve.

PSYCHEDELIC
VISIONS

Psychedelic Visions is for all spiritual seekers who still don't own the video of Fantasia *and refuse to meditate or exercise. Like the Voluptuous Violet (page 106), this smoothie was kept a secret for many years in the interests of public safety. Reactions to this visionary concoction range from "Tart!" and "Kicking" to "Kinky" and "Sweet."*

Yield: 5 cups

4 large mushrooms (shiitake, oyster, or white), diced

4 large strawberries

1 large banana

1 cup orange juice

1/4 cup boysenberry juice

1/4 cup cranberry juice

1. Place all the ingredients in a blender, and blend on medium speed for 1 minute.

2. Pour into tall glasses and serve.

TUTTI-FRUTTI

Discovered in the vaults of the Kremlin after the fall of Communism in the Soviet Union, this recipe had been hermetically sealed in a safe that only the KGB had access to. Even Stalin, the notorious dictator, didn't know of its whereabouts. Perhaps if he had sampled the Tutti-Frutti, he would have been much sweeter and more understanding.

Yield: 4 servings

2 apricots, peeled and sliced

1 nectarine, peeled and sliced

1 cup seedless grapes

1 tablespoon honey

3 cups milk

1 banana

2 tablespoons frozen orange juice concentrate

1. Place all the ingredients in a blender, and blend on medium speed for 30 seconds.

2. Pour into tall glasses and serve.

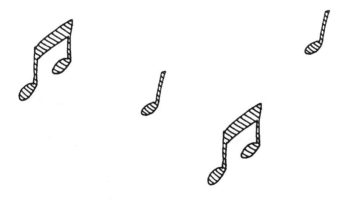

Dangerous Liaisons

This is not a smoothie you want to serve lightly. If you are planning on a divorce, are having an affair, or are even thinking "lustful thoughts," then don't drink this in front of your wife, husband, or significant other. It is quite delicious, and if drunk in excess, it can cause you to reveal your deepest desires to all within shouting distance.

Yield: 4 servings

2 nectarines, peeled, seeded, and sliced

2 cups filtered water

1 banana

1 tablespoon brown rice syrup

2 tablespoons cocoa powder

3 tablespoons frozen orange juice
concentrate

1 1/2 teaspoons tahini

1 tablespoon chocolate syrup

2 ice cubes

1. Place all the ingredients in a blender, and blend on medium speed for 45 seconds.

2. Pour into tall glasses and serve.

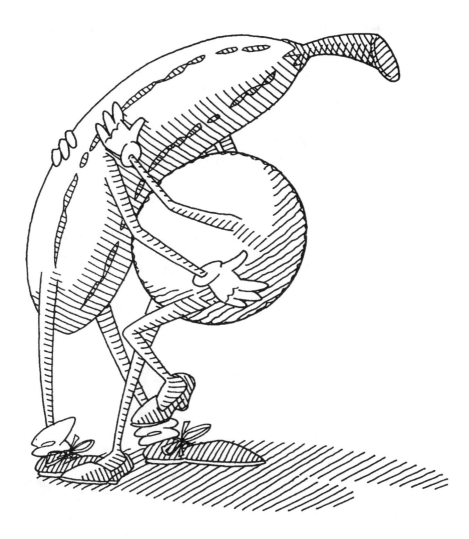

The Peaceful Warrior

Until now, the world was unaware of the day peace almost broke out among the planet's nations. One day, someone tapped into the computers at Air Force Command and put the entire world on alert by entering this smoothie recipe. Before anyone knew what was happening, Russia, China, and the United States were threatening each other with new and exciting smoothies. All weapons of destruction were converted into giant blenders, with a race to see which country could outdo the others in peacetime alternatives and smoothie diversions.

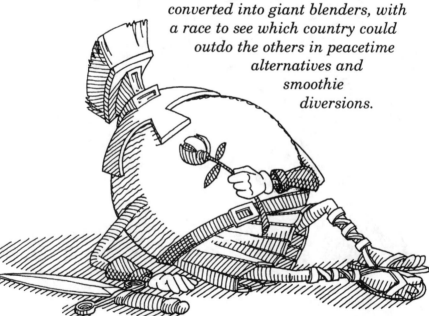

Yield: 4 servings

$1/2$ cantaloupe, peeled, seeded, and sliced

4 ice cubes

2 tablespoons frozen orange juice
concentrate

2 tablespoons vanilla extract

1 plum (European or Japanese), pitted

2 tablespoons maple syrup

$1/2$ cup brown rice syrup

2 tablespoons applesauce

1. Place all the ingredients in a blender, and blend on medium speed for 30 seconds.

2. Pour into tall glasses and serve.

The Shadow

Nobody knows where this smoothie came from or how it was discovered. There is no reference to it in any of the literature or cookbooks in the world, but The Shadow knows . . . it tastes great!

Yield: 4 servings

6 tablespoons frozen orange juice concentrate

3 bananas

2 cups milk

2 tablespoons vanilla extract

8 ice cubes

1. Place all the ingredients in a blender, and mix on medium speed for 30 seconds.

2. Pour into tall glasses and serve.

8.
Animal Dreams

Some people believe in reincarnation, and think we've been born before as people or animals. Some tribes in North and South America believe animals that visit us in our dreams or visions are our guides (totems) who come to give us messages and insights. Still others name their entire community after the "animal people," such as the Raven, Bear, or Eagle Clan. If you were to pick an animal to represent your life spirit, what would it be? If reincarnation exists, what animal would you like to return as?

As you sample these smoothies, try to notice any preferences that may arise. Perhaps you've found your very own totem or animal guide.

THE
Lion Queen

*The lion is the largest cat, second only to the tiger.
To say the lion is strong would be an understatement;
if a lion was pulling a rope in one direction, it would
take at least ten people to pull equally in the opposite
direction. This smoothie is not quite that strong, but
be prepared for the almond extract kick and aftertaste;
it's quite delicious, and stays with you for some time.*

Yield: 4 cups

1 cup firm tofu

2 cups apple juice

2 cups raspberry juice

2 tablespoons raspberry jam

2 ripe bananas

$1/2$ teaspoon almond extract

1. Place all the ingredients in a blender, and mix on medium speed for 30 seconds.

2. Pour into tall glasses and serve.

ORANGUTAN TANG

The orangutan is closely related to the chimpanzee, the gorilla, and humans. Its name comes from two Malay words meaning "man" and "jungle." They enjoy eating fruits and vegetables, and love to play and get into mischief. This smoothie resembles the orangutan in its playfulness and rich, brownish-red color.

Yield: 4 cups

1 1/2 cups rice milk

1 cup plain yogurt

1 banana

1 tablespoon cocoa powder

1/2 teaspoon orange extract

1. Place all the ingredients in a blender, and mix on medium speed for 30 seconds.

2. Pour into tall glasses and serve.

The
Invisible Moose

When you think of Sweden, you think of moose, and you'd expect to find them everywhere, wouldn't you? Not necessarily. My wife and I went there on our honeymoon and stayed with our friends Chris and Eva. They took us to well-known moose locations far and wide, including the king's hunting grounds. They even took us to the zoo in a last, desperate attempt to prove there were indeed moose in Sweden. But the closest we came to seeing moose were the highway signs warning drivers to watch out for them.

You won't have the same problem with The Invisible Moose. It has a unique taste that is unforgettable, and you can make it appear before your delighted eyes as often as you wish.

Yield: 4 cups

1 cup organic oat milk*

1 cup apple juice

1 ripe banana

1 tablespoon honey

* Available at most organic food stores. Soy milk may be substituted.

$^1/_2$ tablespoon nutritional yeast

$^1/_4$ cup sliced almonds

1. Place all the ingredients in a blender, and mix on high speed for 1 minute.

2. Pour into tall glasses and serve.

The
Golden Eagle

Did you know that golden eagles can live for up to fifty years? They need about 9 ounces of food per day, which is about 7 percent of their body weight. You won't need to drink 7 percent of your body weight per day in smoothies, although you may be tempted to do so once you taste The Golden Eagle.

Yield: 4 cups

2 cups water

6 dried apricots, diced

$1/2$ cup raisins

$2 1/2$ ripe bananas

1 teaspoon wheat germ

3 tablespoons light brown sugar

1. Place all the ingredients in a blender, and mix on high speed for 1 minute.

2. Pour into tall glasses and serve.

Leaping
The   Gazelle

Gazelles are one of the oldest mammals in existence—they've been around for over 12 million years! They are admired for their graceful appearance, and have been known to leap as high as twelve feet straight into the air. This smoothie won't make you leap that high, or you'd hit your head on the ceiling, but it will make your insides jump for joy.

Yield: 4 cups

1 cup apricot juice, or 1 cup sliced apricots

1 cup raspberry juice, or 1 cup raspberries

1 cup cranberry juice

1 tablespoon honey

1 ripe banana

1. Place all the ingredients in a blender, and mix on low speed for 15 seconds.

2. Pour into tall glasses and serve.

THE
ELEPHANT'S CHILD

What mammal often lives to be 70 years old and can feed itself, spray water, and lift heavy objects with its long, flexible trunk? The elephant, of course! As you might guess, elephants have a strong sense of smell. They can smell water—or a smoothie—long before they see it. If you practice, you, too, may soon be able to smell The Elephant's Child from afar, but that means drinking smoothies on a daily basis, using proper "smoothie etiquette" at all times.

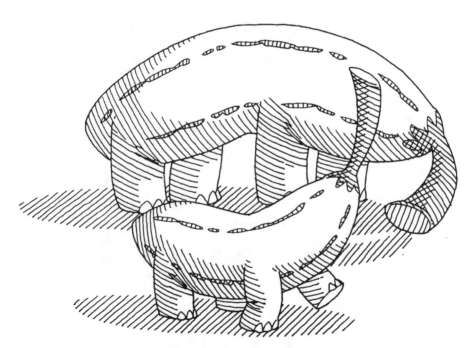

Yield: 3 cups

2 cups soy milk

2 tablespoons peanut butter

2 tablespoons your favorite jelly

1 ripe banana

2 tablespoons honey

2 teaspoons oat bran

1. Place all the ingredients in a blender, and mix on medium speed for 30 seconds.

2. Pour into tall glasses and serve.

Wiley Coyote

The coyote is a North American wild dog closely related to the wolf. Many native peoples have stories and beliefs surrounding the coyote, often referred to as the trickster who outsmarts both friend and foe. Coyotes defend their chosen "territory," howl in chorus, and mate for life. The Wiley Coyote may make you howl, too. As far as mating for life goes, that's another story.

Yield: 4 cups

2 tablespoons raisins

1 ripe banana

1 cup apricot nectar

1 tablespoon carob powder

$1/2$ cup apple juice

$1/2$ cup soy milk

$1/2$ cup firm tofu

1. Place all the ingredients in a blender, and mix on medium speed for 1 minute.

2. Pour into tall glasses and serve.

Masai Giraffe

The giraffe is also known as Giraffa cameleopardalis. *Try saying that clearly ten times in a row. If you've succeeded without blubbering or getting lockjaw, pour yourself a Masai Giraffe to celebrate. These stange-looking creatures (strange to us, not to them) roam the southern areas of East Africa and may reach a height of 18 feet. The Masai Giraffe is a thick, rich, and colorful lunch or supper drink.*

Yield: 2 cups

1 cup sliced, cooked carrots

2 tablespoons raisins

1 cup firm tofu

2 cups soy milk

2 tablespoons brown sugar

1. Place all the ingredients in a blender, and mix on medium speed for 1 minute.

2. Pour into tall glasses and serve.

The Honey Bunny

Bunnies are better known as rabbits or hares. They're cute, cuddly, furry, and wiggle their noses and hop around on large back legs. Everyone loves them. In the wild, they're prey for many birds, and in captivity, they're prey for children who want to snuggle and squeeze them to death. Remember, this drink is not an animal. Do not squeeze it or try to make it hop, or it could get quite messy!

Yield: 4-5 cups

2 ripe bananas

1/3 cup banana-strawberry yogurt (dairy or non-dairy)

1/4 cup firm tofu

3 tablespoons honey

2 cups milk

1. Place all the ingredients in a blender, and mix on medium speed for 45 seconds.

2. Pour into tall glasses and serve.

Smokey Bear

Except for the polar bear, most bears are dark in color and are usually peaceful and timid unless disturbed. If you happen to surprise a bear, especially a mother with cubs, you have two choices. One, slowly back away and act like you don't exist; or two, offer it a Smokey Bear smoothie. This is one of my favorites— cool, refreshing, and filling.

Yield: 4 cups

3 cups soy milk

3 tablespoons carob powder

$1/2$ teaspoon peppermint extract

1 cup firm tofu

2 ripe bananas

2 tablespoons honey

1. Place all the ingredients in a blender, and mix on medium speed for 30 seconds.

2. Place the smoothie mixture in the freezer for 5 minutes, until chilled.

3. Pour into tall glasses and serve.

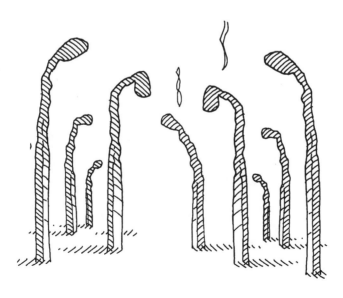

9.
Decadent Desserts

My mother always told me to save dessert for last, so here it is. You could also say, "Keep the best for last," but I wouldn't be surprised to discover that your "inner child" had forced you to turn to this chapter first. That's quite all right. You have the Smoothie Goddess' permission to enjoy these desserts as often as you like, without guilt, remorse, or second-guessing yourself. Yes, some are fattening, but they're also full of protein, vitamins, and that essential ingredient for life—sweetness!

The
Cookie Monster

If you love chocolate chips and peanut butter, then this combination is your cup of tea (or cup of cookie).

Yield: 3 cups

4 tablespoons chocolate chip or carob chip cookie dough (see recipe on page 135)

3 tablespoons creamy peanut butter

2 cups cocoa soy milk, chilled

1 tablespoon honey

1. Place all the ingredients in a blender, and mix on medium speed for one minute.

2. Pour into tall glasses and serve.

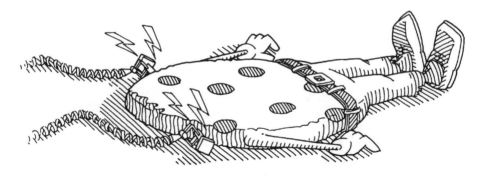

Cookie Dough Recipe

Depending on how many smoothies you make, you should have enough dough left for about half a dozen delicious cookies.

$1\frac{1}{4}$ cups all-purpose flour

$\frac{1}{2}$ teaspoon baking powder

$\frac{1}{8}$ teaspoon salt

$\frac{1}{2}$ cup unsalted butter or soy margarine

$\frac{1}{2}$ cup granulated sugar

$1\frac{1}{2}$ teaspoons egg replacer, or 1 egg

2 tablespoons water

1 teaspoon vanilla extract

$1\frac{1}{4}$ cups chocolate chips or carob chips

1. Mix the flour, baking powder, and salt in a bowl.

2. In a large bowl, cream together the butter or margarine and the sugar. Add the egg replacer, water, and vanilla extract.

3. Mix the dry ingredients with the wet ingredients. Add the chocolate or carob chips, and blend well.

4. Drop rounded teaspoonfuls of dough onto a cookie sheet, placing them about $1\frac{1}{2}$ inches apart.

5. Bake at 350°F for 10-15 minutes. Transfer the cookies to a wire rack and cool completely

A La Mode

This smoothie combines apple pie and ice cream in one luscious package. It's delicious and good for any occasion.

Yield: 4$^1/_2$ cups

3 cups apple juice

3 apples, peeled, seeded, and diced

1 $^1/_2$ teaspoons lemon juice

$^3/_4$ cup raisins

6 tablespoons maple syrup

$^3/_4$ teaspoon nutmeg

3 teaspoons cinnamon

$^3/_4$ cup granola

6 tablespoons vanilla ice cream

1. Place all the ingredients in a blender, and blend on medium speed for 45 seconds.

2. Pour into tall glasses and serve.

The Georgia Peach

Some of the best things in life are simple, and this is one of them. Georgia, long known as the Peach State, will surely make this smoothie their state drink. Legislation is now pending in Atlanta.

Yield: 3 cups

1 ¹/₂ cups peach nectar

1 ¹/₂ cups orange juice

1. Place all the ingredients in a blender, and blend on low speed for 15 seconds.

2. Serve over ice in tall glasses.

The
Gingerbread Man

The verdict is in on this smoothie. It only took the jury one minute to reach a unanimous decision: The Gingerbread Man is guilty on all counts. "Intense, delicious, different, wickedly wonderful, and strange," ruled the judge.

Yield: 4 cups

$3/4$ teaspoon ground ginger

2 tablespoons powdered chocolate spirulina

$1/2$ teaspoon cinnamon

2 cups soy milk

$3/4$ cup crushed graham crackers
(about 3-5 crackers)

1. Place all the ingredients in a blender, and blend on high speed for 30 seconds.

2. Pour into tall glasses and serve.

JASON'S ROOT BEER JUBILEE

My son Jason invented this one (minus the protein powder). It's a root beer float with an added twist— healthy ingredients for everyone's benefit. (But they don't have to know that!)

Yield: 5 cups

1 1/2 teaspoons protein powder

1 cup vanilla ice cream

1/2 cup vanilla yogurt

1 frozen banana (see page 36)

1 12-ounce can root beer

1. Place all the ingredients, except the root beer, in a blender, and blend on medium speed for 20 seconds.

2. Add the root beer, and blend on low speed for 5 seconds.

3. Pour into tall glasses and serve.

Mom's Apple Pie

A traditional, all-American drink. For a Norman Rockwell, "Father Knows Best" kind of family treat, like Mom's apple pie, try this smoothie.

Yield: 3 cups

2 baked apples*

1 teaspoon cinnamon

1/4 cup brown rice syrup or honey

1 1/2 cups filtered water

1. Place all the ingredients in a blender, and blend on medium speed for 30 seconds.

2. Pour into tall glasses and serve.

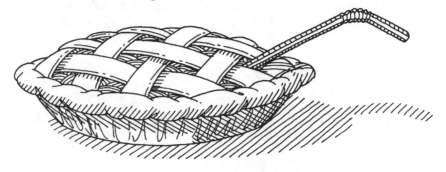

* Bake apples at 350°F for 10-15 minutes, or until soft.

Cavity Rampage

This smoothie is decadence incarnate; it will satisfy anyone's sweet tooth!

Yield: 4$\frac{1}{2}$ cups

1 tablespoon honey

$\frac{1}{2}$ cup raspberries

$\frac{1}{4}$ cup chocolate or carob chips

1 tablespoon vanilla extract

$\frac{1}{2}$ cup broken peanut brittle

3 small bananas

2 cups sparkling mineral water

1. Place all the ingredients, except the sparkling water, in a blender, and mix on high speed for 1 minute.

2. Add the sparkling mineral water and stir.

3. Pour into tall glasses and serve.

SUPER SLUSH

When I was a kid, we used to get drinks at carnivals and sporting events called "slushees," which were essentially crushed ice, sugar, and fruit juice. The Super Slush has a similar consistency, but with a hundred times better ingredients and taste.

Yield: 4½ cups

1 cup ice cream, any flavor*

½ cup plain yogurt

2 small frozen bananas (see page 36)

¼ cup shaved ice

1 cup milk (dairy or non-dairy)

1 teaspoon vanilla extract

½ cup raspberries, blackberries, or strawberries

1. Place all the ingredients in a blender, and mix on medium speed for 1 minute.

2. Pour into tall glasses and serve.

*For a special treat, use homemade ice cream.

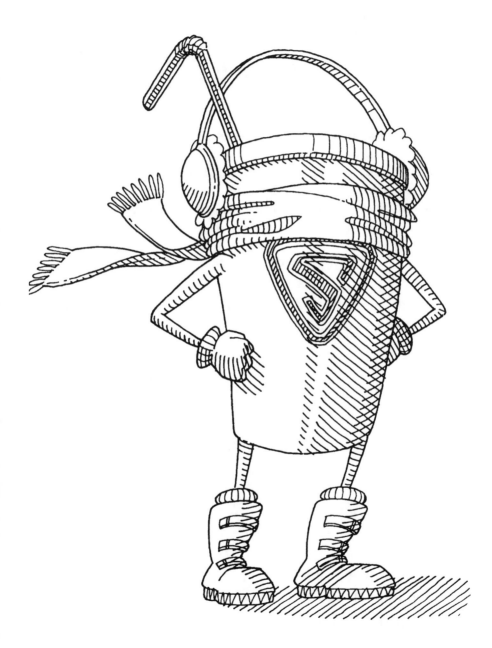

PINK The FLAMINGO

Take a drink of this smoothie and try to not think about pink flamingos. Impossible, you say? Perhaps, but not as difficult as avoiding the image of a pink elephant.

Yield: 4 cups

1 cup raspberry juice

4 tablespoons frozen orange juice

1 cup filtered water

3 small bananas

2 tablespoons plain yogurt

$1/4$ cup firm tofu

10 fresh strawberries

1 cup peeled and chopped cantaloupe

1. Place all ingredients in a blender, and mix on medium speed for 40 seconds.

2. Pour into tall glasses and serve.

Index